A Personal Journey with Martin Scorsese Through American Movies

MARTIN SCORSESE AND MICHAEL HENRY WILSON

faber and faber

bfi

A CIP record for this book
is available from the British Library

ISBN: 0-571-19242-4 (cased)
0-571-19455-9 (paperback)

2 4 6 8 10 9 7 5 3 1

Page 2: Frank Sinatra and Shirley MacLaine in Vincente Minnelli's *Some Came Running*.

CONTENTS

Preface 7

Introduction 13

1 The Director's Dilemma 19

2 The Director as Storyteller 31

The Western 35 The Gangster Film 47 The Musical 59

3 The Director as Illusionist 67

4 The Director as Smuggler 97

5 The Director as Iconoclast 135

Conclusion 165

Filmography 169

Credits 190

So I borrowed it from the New York Public Library, repeatedly.

A Pictorial History of the Movies by Deems Taylor was a year-by-year history of the movies in black and white stills, up to 1949. That book cast a spell on me. I hadn't seen many of the films described in the book, so all I had at my disposal to experience them were these black and white stills. I would fantasize about them, they would play into my dreams. And I was so tempted to steal some of these pictures. A terrible urge—it was a library book after all! I confess: once or twice, I did give in to that urge.

I remember quite clearly—it was 1946 and I was four years old—when my mother took me to see King Vidor's *Duel in the Sun*. I was fanatical about Westerns. My father usually took me to see them, but this time my mother did. The movie had been condemned by the Church. "Lust in the Dust," they dubbed it. I guess she used me as an excuse to see it herself.

From the opening titles I was mesmerized. The bright blasts of deliriously vibrant color, the gunshots, the savage intensity of the music, the burning sun, the overt sexuality. A flawed film, maybe. Yet the hallucinatory quality of the imagery has never weakened for me over the years.

Jennifer Jones played a half-breed servant girl and Gregory Peck was the villain, a ruthless rancher's son who seduced her. For a child this was puzzling. How could the heroine fall for the villain? It was all quite overpowering. Frightening too. The final "duel in the sun," where Jennifer Jones shoots Gregory Peck, was too intense for this four-year-old. I covered my eyes through most of it. It seemed that the two protagonists could only consummate their passion by killing each other.

I didn't know it then, but in 1946 Hollywood had reached its zenith. Two decades later, when I embraced filmmaking, the studio system had collapsed and movie companies were taken over by giant corporations. But it was during the fifties that my passion for films grew and became a vocation. The movies then were entering a new era, the era of *The Searchers* and *The Girl Can't Help It*, *East of Eden* and *Blackboard Jungle*, *Bigger Than Life* and *Vertigo*.

My passion was fueled by all sorts of famous and infamous films—not necessarily the culturally correct ones. By films you may never have heard of: *The Naked Kiss*, *The Phenix City Story*, *The Red House* (page 16) and *Murder by Contract* (below). And by directors who are sadly forgotten: Allan Dwan, Samuel Fuller, Phil Karlson, Ida Lupino, Delmer Daves, André de Toth, Joseph H. Lewis, Irving Lerner.

SCENE: "I DON'T LIKE PIGS."

Claude (Vince Edwards), the contract killer who only believes in dollars and cents, is a mystery—even to his mentors. "I'm different," he claims. "I don't make mistakes. I eliminate personal feelings." His employer, Mr. Moon (Michael Granger) finds him too smart, too cool.

Mr. Moon *(standing by the fireplace)*: Don't you get restless?

Claude *(sitting)*: If I get restless, I exercise. My girl lives in Cleveland.

Mr. Moon: Well, this is not Cleveland.

Claude: I don't like pigs.

Mr. Moon: I do. Human nature.

IRVING LERNER: *MURDER BY CONTRACT* (1958)

MARTIN SCORSESE Over the years, I have discovered many obscure films and sometimes these were more inspirational than the prestigious films that received all the attention. I can't really be objective. I can only revisit what has moved or

Duel in the Sun (1946): Brilliant color and delirious music intensify the passion between Gregory Peck and Jennifer Jones.

Overlooked Films:
Samuel Fuller's *The Naked Kiss* (top),
Phil Karlson's *The Phenix City Story*
(middle) and Delmer Daves's
The Red House (bottom).

Sullivan's Travels (1941): Preston Sturges tells the story of a director (Joel McCrea, center) struggling between art and commerce.

intrigued me. This is a journey inside an imaginary museum, unfortunately one too big for us to enter each room. There is too much to see, too much to remember! So I've chosen to highlight some of the films that colored my dreams, that changed my perceptions, and in some cases even my life. Films that prompted me, for better or for worse, to become a filmmaker myself.

As early as I can remember, the key issue for me was: What does it take to be a filmmaker in Hollywood? Even today I still wonder what it takes to be a professional or even an artist in Hollywood. How do you survive the constant tug of war between personal expression and commercial imperatives? What is the price you pay to work in Hollywood? Do you end up with a split personality? Do you make one movie for them, one for yourself?

SCENE: ART VERSUS COMMERCE
John L. Sullivan (Joel McCrea) is a successful director who has never made a serious film. His comedies were trifles, with such titles as So Long, Sarong *and* Ants in Your Plants of 1939. *When he decides to make "a message picture, a commentary on modern conditions, a true canvas of the suffering of humanity," his producer, Mr. Hadrian (Porter Hall), and the studio head, Mr. LeBrand (Robert Warwick), think he has lost his mind. They surround Sullivan and attempt to reason him.*

Mr. Hadrian: How about making *Ants in Your Plants of 1941*? You can have Bob Hope, Mary Martin.

Mr. Le Brand: Maybe Bing Crosby.

Hadrian: The Abbey Dancers.

Le Brand: Maybe Jack Benny and Rochester.

Hadrian: A big name band and . . .

Sullivan *(coming out of his trance)*: What? Oh no, I want to make *Oh Brother, Where Art Thou*?

PRESTON STURGES: *SULLIVAN'S TRAVELS* (1941)

1

THE DIRECTOR'S

DILEMMA

King Vidor in the editing room.

The Crowd (1928): James Murray in King Vidor's unusual pre-Depression drama.

obsessive perfectionist who wanted to top his greatest achievement, *Gone with the Wind*, made seven years earlier.

GREGORY PECK The result was a kind of grandiose quality. It was a bit over the top. Take the barroom scene. There never was such a bar in the West. It was about the size of Madison Square Garden, and almost Oriental in its lavishness.

But to David it was great fun to exaggerate, to heighten. He was having the time of his life. His all-encompassing enthusiasm galvanized everybody. That energy, that sense of playfulness, of rascality—that was Selznick. About one o'clock or two o'clock in the morning, when the actors had to go to sleep, David would settle down and rewrite the script. And we'd get different colored pages the next morning. That didn't always sit well with the directors, but it was David's picture. It was his baby and things were done his way.

The great King Vidor was directing, but David was overcome by his own enthusiasm at times and began more and more to direct over King's shoulder. And that created considerable tension on the set, finally leading to the moment when King stood up somewhere out in Tucson and told David that he knew what he could do with the picture and walked off. William Dieterle finished the picture.

MARTIN SCORSESE Somehow, Vidor survived as an on-again, off-again team player. He even worked again later on with Selznick in television. Vidor was probably the most resilient of the film pioneers—one of the few who were able, time and again, to convince the moguls to let them experiment with the medium. Throughout his career, he succeeded in alternating studio assignments—pictures like *The Champ* and *Stella*

Dallas, with personal projects like *Hallelujah*, *Our Daily Bread* and *The Crowd* (page 22), a most unusual pre-Depression drama. MGM's Irving Thalberg agreed to finance *The Crowd* because Vidor had given the studio its greatest success of the silent era, *The Big Parade*. Sometimes to get his movies produced, Vidor was even willing to mortgage his house or gamble his own salary. Somehow *he* found a way to make one for the studios, one for himself.

The Hollywood of the classical era—the thirties and forties—was based on a powerful, vertically integrated industry. The studios, particularly the five "majors" (MGM, Warner Bros., Paramount, RKO, and Fox) controlled every phase of the process: production, distribution, even exhibition as they owned their own chains of theaters worldwide. To produce fifty pictures a year, each studio held its stars, writers, directors, producers, and an army of skilled technicians, under long-term contracts. They even cultivated a recognizable style, a certain "look" in their films.

GREGORY PECK MGM was more of a dream world, where everything was idealized and somewhat sentimentalized. That came, I think, from L. B. Mayer—what he thought was classy. And Fox leaned more toward, I wouldn't say exactly gritty realism because they made Betty Grable musicals, ice skating pictures, and all kinds of pictures, but toward the things that Zanuck is remembered for—pictures with a social conscience done with a degree of realism. This would probably not be characteristic of MGM.

BILLY WILDER In those days I could look at a picture and if everything was in white silk—MGM! I could look at a picture and if it was Fred

Duel in the Sun (1946): Gregory Peck and Lionel Barrymore look incredulous at producer David Selznick's latest idea.

The Studio Look: In Hollywood's golden era, each studio had an identifiable style. *Camille* (left) shows MGM's idealized world; *Public Enemy* (top), the gritty look of Warner Bros.; and *The Grapes of Wrath* (bottom) is an example of the "social conscience" at Fox.

2

THE DIRECTOR
AS STORYTELLER

MARTIN SCORSESE "If you haven't got the story, you haven't got anything!" Raoul Walsh used to say. This is a cardinal rule in moviemaking. The American filmmaker has always been more interested in creating fiction than in revealing reality. Early on, the documentary form was discarded or relegated to marginal status. For better or for worse, the Hollywood director is an entertainer; he is in the business of telling stories. He is therefore saddled with conventions and stereotypes, formulas and clichés, limitations which were codified in specific genres. This was the very foundation of the studio system.

Audiences loved genre pictures and the old masters never seemed reluctant to supply them. When John Ford rose in the middle of a tempestuous meeting at the Directors Guild of America in 1950, this is how he introduced himself: "My name is John Ford. I make Westerns." He was not referring to his more honored pictures such as *The Informer* or *The Grapes of Wrath*, *How Green Was My Valley* or *The Quiet Man*. His Westerns were what he was most proud of—or so he may have wanted us to believe.

Eventually, film genres would serve to organize assembly-line production: each studio made so many Westerns, so many musicals, and so many gangster films. It all started with Edwin Porter's *The Great Train Robbery*. This was one of the first attempts at scripting a story. Fittingly, it also was a Western.

The first master storyteller of the American screen was D. W. Griffith. His sensibility was steeped in a literary tradition, that of Dickens and Tolstoy, Frank Norris and Walt Whitman. Yet while borrowing from 19th century literature, Griffith was forging the new art of the 20th century. He explored the emotional impact of film and before the outbreak of World War I had

The Great Train Robbery (1903): Edwin S. Porter's Western was one of the first attempts at scripting a story.

already delineated nearly every genre, even the gangster film with his short *The Musketeers of Pig Alley*.

Genres were never rigid. Creative filmmakers kept stretching their boundaries. This was a classical art where personal expression was stimulated rather than inhibited by discipline. Take Raoul Walsh, the most gifted apprentice and disciple of Griffith. His strongest films were variations on a few themes and characters. The figure of the sympathetic outlaw, for instance, a rebel in the tradition of Jesse James, inspired him time and again. In *High Sierra*, you didn't root for the police and the ordinary citizens. You rooted for the gangster. And you knew he was doomed when he became separated from the only person who cared about him, his tarnished angel, Ida Lupino.

At the end of his memoirs, Walsh quoted Shakespeare, his constant inspiration: "Each man in his time plays many parts." This applies not only to Walsh himself, but also to his explosive characters. These outcasts were bigger than life. They stood beyond good and evil. Their lust for life was insatiable, even as their actions precipitated their tragic destiny. The world was too small for them and Walsh often gave them a cosmic battleground: Mount Whitney and the High Sierras.

Eight years after *High Sierra*, Walsh filmed *Colorado Territory*, the same story as a Western. Again he provided his desperado with a wide landscape which dwarfed human figures, this time the City of the Moon and the Canyon of Death. So dear to Walsh's heart was his heroine, now a half-breed outcast, that he gave her as much strength and character as the hero.

You might even sense a mystical dimension at the end of the film that clearly transcended any genre limitation. The lost city is like a primitive cathedral and as he listens to the Navajos chanting in the night, Joel McCrea reflects on his fate and appears to accept it. Walsh used some of the same camera angles as in *High Sierra*. But this time the messenger of death was a Navajo sharpshooter. And in *Colorado Territory*, the tragedy was complete: both protagonists were doomed.

The most interesting of the classic movie genres to me are the indigenous ones: the Western, which was born on the Frontier, the Gangster Film, which originated in the East Coast cities, and the Musical, which was spawned by Broadway. They remind me of jazz: they allowed for endless, increasingly complex, sometimes perverse variations. When these variations were played by the masters, they reflected the changing times; they gave you fascinating insights into American culture and the American psyche.

Walsh's Sympathetic Outlaws and Strong Heroines: Humphrey Bogart and Ida Lupino in *High Sierra* (top) and Joel McCrea and Virginia Mayo in *Colorado Territory* (bottom).

The Savage Violence of the Western:
Robert Ryan and Janet Leigh in Anthony Mann's *The Naked Spur*

The Western

MARTIN SCORSESE You can see how a genre evolved just by watching three Westerns John Ford directed with the same actor, John Wayne. The character of the hero becomes richer, more complex, with each decade.

The Ringo Kid of *Stagecoach* (1939) grows first into the benevolent father figure of *She Wore a Yellow Ribbon* (1949). Then Ford transforms him into Ethan Edwards, the misfit of *The Searchers* (1956), who returns from years of wandering to discover that his loved ones have been massacred by the Indians. John Wayne's heroic "persona" has turned dark and obsessive. The physical death of the Indian is not enough. Ethan wants to ensure his spiritual death as well.

SCENE: **A SPIRITUAL DEATH**

The Reverend (Ward Bond) and his posse have found the burial site of a Comanche. With the help of Charlie (Ken Curtis), the Reverend removes the flat boulder and reveals the corpse in a shallow grave. A hand removes the scarf that covers the Indian's face. Ethan Edwards (John Wayne) remains on his horse, at a distance.

Charlie: This one has come a long way before he died, Captain.

Reverend *(to Ethan)*: Well, Ethan, there's another one you can score up for your brother.

(Overcome by grief, young Brad Jorgensen played by Harry Carey, Jr. smashes a large rock into the grave.)

Reverend: Jorgensen!

Ethan *(pulling his gun)*: Why don't you finish the job?

(He fires at the dead Comanche off-screen. Then he fires a second shot.)

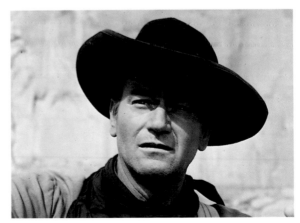

Ford's Transformation of the Western Hero: John Wayne as a cocky kid in *Stagecoach* (top), a kindly father figure in *She Wore a Yellow Ribbon* (middle), and an obsessive misfit in *The Searchers*.

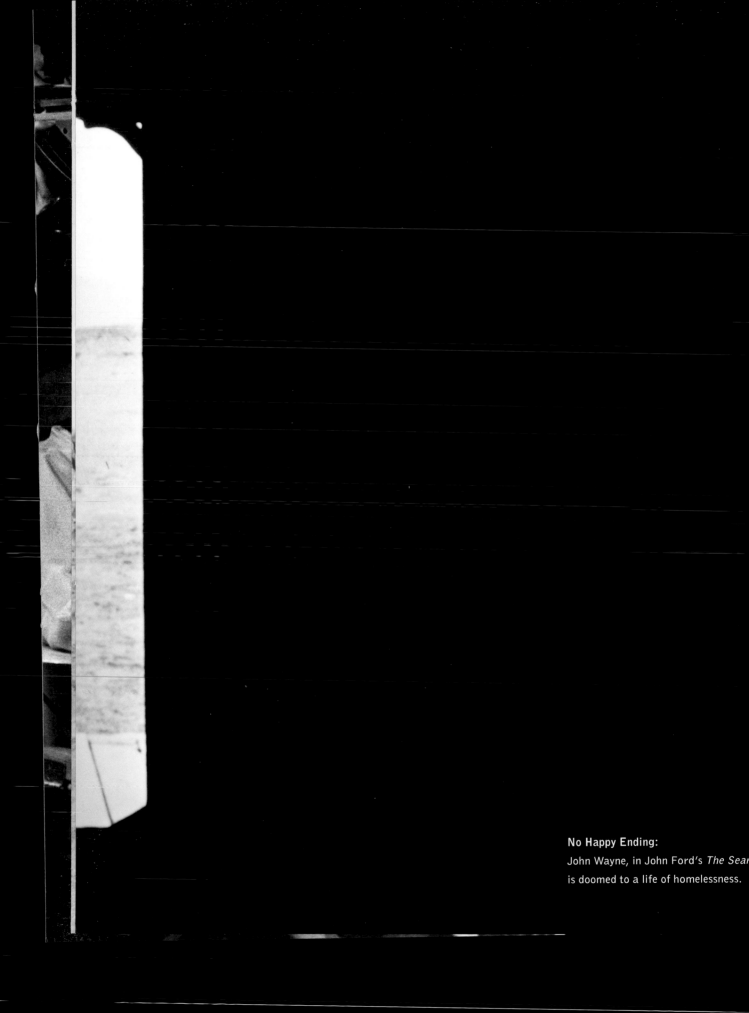

No Happy Ending:
John Wayne, in John Ford's *The Sea*
is doomed to a life of homelessness.

The Roaring Twenties (1939):
Gladys George cradling the dying
James Cagney in this semireligious
image at the end of Walsh's movie.

A Landscape of Moral Conflicts: John Garfield in *Force of Evil.*

was unusually poetic, but what you saw was a world of sleaze and greed imploding before your eyes. The system's violence became the issue rather than individual violence.

SCENE: "DYING WHILE YOU ARE BREATHING"
Sitting down in a New York diner, Leo Morse (Thomas Gomez) faces his accountant Freddie Bauer (Howland Chamberlain).

Leo Morse: I'm glad you called me, Freddie. I'm glad you thought it over to listen to me. To calm down and listen to me so I can help you. *(To waiter)* Coffee.

Freddie Bauer: Please, Mr. Morse, all I want is to quit. That's all. Nothing else. They won't let me quit and I want to quit. I'll die if I don't quit.

Leo Morse: I'm a man with heart trouble. I die almost every day myself. That's the way I live. Silly habit! You know, sometimes you feel as though you're dying here *(he touches his pulse)* and here *(touches his fingers)* and here *(touches his heart)*, you're dying while you are breathing.

(Hearing that a car has pulled in front of the diner, he turns toward the door, still holding his coffee cup.)

Leo Morse *(realizing that he has been betrayed)*: Freddie, what have you done? Freddie! What have you done to me?

(Two of the gangsters pull Leo by the arms.)

Gangster #1: Take it easy, Pop. You won't get hurt.

Gangster #2: You're safe with us, Pop. C'mon, you can't take all night. Stand up and walk! *(As they start dragging him out, Freddy Bauer runs for the exit.)*

Gangster #3: Stop him! *(Freddie is tripped by one of the assailants and falls on his back, losing his glasses.)*

Gangster #3 *(yelling hysterically)*: He knows me. Kill him, kill him, he knows me!

(He seizes a gun from one of his men and aims at the accountant's face. The dying man sees the gangster firing at him point blank. Leo is dragged to the car.)

ABRAHAM POLONSKY: *FORCE OF EVIL* (1948)

breast-pocket), now, I want simple answers. Dave, no diagrams. Dink's got the full say around here, right?

Accountant: Yes.

Frankie: Okay then . . .

Accountant: Except that it's revocable by a vote of the board of directors of Reeds and Associates.

Frankie: Stop the double talk.

Accountant: I'm sorry, Frankie.

Frankie *(exasperated)*: Just what does Dink own?

Accountant: In which corporation?

(In frustration, Frankie looks up at Dink and turns around, totally perplexed.)

BYRON HASKIN: *I WALK ALONE* (1948)

MARTIN SCORSESE Some films, notably Abraham Polonsky's *Force of Evil* (1948), went even further and painted the whole society as corrupt. The face of John Garfield, a lawyer for the mob, was a landscape of moral conflicts. The social body itself was sick. Polonsky's dialogue

Force of Evil (1948): The mob expected its members to sacrifice their families. Thomas Gomez is taken by his brother's criminal associates.

Behind The Scenes: William Wellman directs James Cagney and Edward Woods on the street (left, top) in *Public Enemy*. The finished scenes on film: a machine gun operated by rival gangsters (left, bottom), and Woods being shot (above).

42nd Street (1933): Warner Baxter as the obsessed Broadway producer in
Busby Berkeley's backstage musical, a show-biz figure who burns himself out.

Goldiggers of 1933 (1933): Berkeley realized that a movie musical was different from a staged musical: the camera was part of the choreography in Leroy's movie.

3

THE DIRECTOR

AS ILLUSIONIST

MARTIN SCORSESE Of course, it is not enough for the director to be just a storyteller. To implement his vision, he has to be a technician and even an illusionist. This means controlling and mastering the technical process. Our palette has expanded tremendously through a century of constant experimentations as the movies grew from silent to sound, black and white to Technicolor, standard screen size to Cinemascope, 35mm to 70mm. The American movie industry, it seems, never failed to embrace new technological developments. Somehow, it moved faster and more decisively than its foreign rivals.

As King Vidor said, "The cinema is the greatest means of expression ever invented. But it is an illusion more powerful than any other and it should therefore be in the hands of the magicians and wizards who can bring it to life."

Buster Keaton may have had the same thought when he made *The Cameraman*. His character was actually that of an aspiring cameraman. In the hope of getting a job he showed his footage to MGM executives. Unfortunately, he had double-exposed the film: divers were leaping in reverse, a battleship cruised down 5th Avenue, cars and trucks collided in an urban kaleidoscope. . . The screening was a disaster. However, as every director will experience, accidents can be the source of extraordinary poetry and beauty. All that Keaton's cameraman needed was to learn and master the language of film.

Interestingly, most of the early film pioneers, including D. W. Griffith, had no formal education. They were self-taught and often shared the prevailing prejudice that the cinema was a minor form of entertainment. The American film probably came of age in February 1915 when Griffith opened his first feature-length epic, *The Birth of a Nation*.

According to Raoul Walsh, who was one of Griffith's assistants at the time and who played the role of John Wilkes Booth, it took *The Birth of a Nation* to convince Americans that "films were an art in their own right and not just the illegitimate offspring of the theater." How did Griffith achieve this triumph? Essentially through his composition and orchestration of the shots. As Walsh put it: "The high and low angle shots turned a good picture into a great one." One close-up was worth a thousand words. Erich von Stroheim, also one of Griffith's assistants, acknowledged that he was "the pioneer of filmdom, the first to put beauty and poetry into a cheap and tawdry sort of amusement."

I have always felt that visual literacy is just as important as verbal literacy. What the film pioneers were exploring was the medium's specific techniques. In the process, they invented a new language based on images rather than words, a visual grammar you might say: close-ups, irises, dissolves, masking part of the frame for emphasis, dolly shots, tracking shots. These are the basic tools that directors have at their disposal to create and heighten the illusion of reality. When Lillian Gish called D. W. Griffith the father of film, she used the same analogy: "He gave us the grammar of filmmaking. He understood the psychic strength of the lens."

Half a century later, Stanley Kubrick may have had Griffith in mind when he remarked that what is truly original in the art of filmmaking, what distinguishes it from all the other arts, may be the editing process. As a matter of fact, the technique of cross-cutting was developed by Griffith two years before *The Birth of a Nation*. In *Death's Marathon*, for instance, a 1913 short film, he shows you two events happening simultaneously and intercuts them to increase the

The Cameraman (1928): Buster Keaton as a cameraman
learning to master the language of film in Sedgwick's movie.

The Birth of a Nation (1915): Griffith's composition and orchestration of such shots
as these featuring Henry B. Walthall (top) and Raoul Walsh playing John Wilkes Booth
(bottom) convinced Americans that film was an art in its own right.

suspense. At the time, Griffith had to fight his distributors who feared that audiences would be confused by such an innovation.

It was in the great epics of the silent era that the illusionists learned to use special effects and visual wizardry to conjure up some of their most compelling visions. The American tradition of the great spectacle was born circa 1915, when Griffith saw *Cabiria*, an Italian superproduction. Giovanni Pastrone's *Cabiria* had all the right ingredients: adventure, melodrama, pageantry, religion, extraordinary production design, and striking camera angles and lighting. To film the crossing of the Alps, they actually had to drag Hannibal's elephants up onto a mountain top.

Reportedly, Griffith watched it twice in one night. It inspired him; it gave him the audacity to create his masterpiece, *Intolerance*. Much has been made of the epic production's extravagant budget, real-size sets and thousands of extras. Griffith's achievement is all the more extraordinary because he worked without a script. It was all planned in his head—not on paper. But Griffith went even further in his experiments. *Intolerance* was a daring attempt at interweaving stories and characters, not from the same period, but from four different centuries. Freely cross-cutting from one era to another, he blended them all together in a grand symphony devoted to one idea—a passionate plea for tolerance.

Griffith's passion for history was balanced by his passion for simple people, the victims of history. In the episode set in modern-day America, a young woman is deemed an unfit mother because her husband is in jail (page 72). Oppression is represented by society matrons, puritan Reformers who want to place her baby in an orphanage. Griffith's distressed heroines— Mae Marsh as the Dear One, Constance Talmadge

Cabiria (1914): Giovanni Pastrone's melodramatic spectacle with its grand production design and striking lighting was an influence on Griffith.

Intolerance (1916): With interweaving stories (the St. Bartholomew Massacre, above) from different time periods, Griffith made his grandiose movie without a script.

Intolerance (1916): Mae Marsh in the modern-day American episode of Griffith's movie, an eloquent close-up of one of his victims of history.

Sunrise (1927): Murnau offered visions rather than plot with such images of George O'Brien with Margaret Livingstone as a vamp, the city girl (left, top) who tempted the young farmer to drown his wife Janet Gaynor (left, bottom). Later the broken couple is reunited (above).

Her Man (1930): With fluid camera moves, Garnett skillfully choreographs this fistfight in a honkytonk bar (Ricardo Cortez at center in pin–stripe suit).

Leave Her to Heaven (1945): A film noir
in color. The brilliant Technicolor enhanced
this melodrama in which Gene Tierney plays
a neurotic, possessive woman.

The Fall of the Roman Empire (1964): In one of the last great epics, which became too expensive to make, Mann shows a masterful sense of space and dramatic composition.

4

THE DIRECTOR

AS SMUGGLER

Simone Simon and Tom Conway in Jacques Tourneur's *Cat People*.

MARTIN SCORSESE We have looked at the rules, at the narrative codes, at the technical tools. And have seen how Hollywood filmmakers adjusted to these limitations; they even played with them. Now is the time to look at the cracks in the system.

What slipped through these cracks has always fascinated me. There were opportunities, there were projects that allowed for the expression of different sensibilities, offbeat themes, or even radical political views—particularly when the financial stakes were minimal. Less money, more freedom! The world of B-films was often freer and more conducive to experimenting and innovating. Directors in the forties found that they could exercise more control on a small budget movie than on a prestigious A-picture. Also, they had fewer executives looking over their shoulder. They could introduce unusual touches, weave unexpected motifs, and sometimes transform routine material into a much more personal expression. In a sense, they became smugglers. They cheated and somehow got away with it.

Style was crucial. The first master of esoterica was Jacques Tourneur, who began making his mark in low-budget supernatural thrillers. On *Cat People*, he had a good reason not to show the creature. "The less you see, the more you believe," he stated. "You must never try to impose your views on the viewer, but rather you must try to let it seep in, little by little." This oblique approach perfectly defines the smuggler's strategy.

The son of pioneer filmmaker Maurice Tourneur, Jacques Tourneur had the good fortune to find an extraordinary oasis of creative subversion in producer Val Lewton's unit at RKO. Lewton, a former story editor for Selznick, was once described as "a benevolent David Selznick." He worked extensively on all of the scripts that he

Master of Esoterica: Jacques Tourneur (left) on the set of *Cat People.*

produced, but he never set foot on the set and left the director to his own devices.

SCENE: **THE UNSEEN**

Walking along a park late at night, Alice (Jane Randolph) appears to be stalked by an unseen presence. She turns to look back, but the street is deserted. She walks faster. A loud hiss makes her jump. It is only a municipal bus pulling up. Yet above her, some branches move ominously.

Bus driver: Climb on, sister. Are you riding with me or ain't you? *(After she steps in)* You look as if you'd seen a ghost.

Alice *(livid):* Did you see it?

(The driver shakes his head. She pays her fare. The bus leaves. In the park, the same branches appear to be moving slightly.)

JACQUES TOURNEUR: *CAT PEOPLE* (1942)

MARTIN SCORSESE A B-film like *Cat People* only cost $134,000, but it touched a chord in America by venturing into hitherto unexplored territory: a young bride's fear of her own sexual-

Cat People (1942): In Tourneur's films the characters are not in control of their lives. Simone Simon is consumed by malevolent feline spirits.

Bennett), the prostitute he has been keeping and for whom he has embezzled company funds. He runs to her boudoir, convinced that she will choose him over her conman lover Johnny. She is on her bed in a negligée.

Kitty: Why did you come here?

Christopher: To ask you to marry me.

Kitty: What about your wife?

Christopher: I haven't any wife. That's finished.

Kitty: For God's sake, you didn't . . .

Christopher: Her husband turned up. I'm free. *(She buries her face in a pillow.)* I don't care what's happened. I can marry you now. I want you to be my wife. We'll go away together. Way far off so you can forget this other man. Please don't cry, Kitty.

Kitty *(rising and facing him)*: I'm not crying, you fool. I'm laughing.

Christopher: Kitty!

Kitty: Oh, you idiot. How can a man be so dumb!

Christopher: Kitty!!

(Shocked, he steps back and bumps into the ice bucket. He picks up the ice pick.)

Kitty: I wanted to laugh in your face ever since I first met you. You're old and ugly and I'm sick of you. Sick, sick, sick!

Christopher: Kitty, for Heaven's sake!

Kitty *(sitting defiantly with her hands on her hips)*: You kill Johnny? I'd like to see you try. Why, he'd break every bone in your body. He's a man. You wanna marry me? You? Get out of here! Get out! Get away from me. *(As he moves menacingly toward her with the ice pick)* Chris! Chris! Get away from me! Chris! Chris!

(She tries to hide under the bed covers. He stabs her repeatedly.)

FRITZ LANG: *SCARLET STREET* (1945)

FRITZ LANG (1967) Violence has become, in my opinion, a definite point in a script. It has a dramaturgical reason to be there. I don't think people believe in the devil with the horns and the forked tail and therefore they don't believe in punishment after they are dead. So the question was for me: What do people believe? What are people fearing? That is physical pain. And physical pain comes from violence. That I think is today the only thing that people really fear. And therefore it has become a definite part of life and naturally also of scripts.

MARTIN SCORSESE The phrase "film noir" was coined by the French critics in 1946, when they discovered the Hollywood productions they had missed during the German occupation. This was not a specific genre like the Gangster Film, but rather a mood which was best described by this line from Edward G. Ulmer's *Detour:* "Which ever way you turn, fate sticks out its foot to trip you."

SCENE: **HAUNTED MEMORY**

Al Roberts (Tom Neal) recalls his nightmare when he hears the jukebox in a Las Vegas diner:

Voice-over: Did you ever wanna forget anything? Did you ever want to cut away a piece of your memory or blot it out? You can't, you know, no matter how hard you try. You can change the scenery, but sooner or later you'll get a whiff of perfume or somebody will say a certain phrase, or maybe hum something. Then you're licked again.

EDGAR G. ULMER: *DETOUR* (1946)

MARTIN SCORSESE In *Detour*, down-and-out pianist Tom Neal hitchhikes his way West to join his fiancée. His life starts unraveling when the man who has given him a lift dies unexpectedly. Doom was written on Tom Neal's face. He was bewildered, and afraid to go to the police. Keeping the dead man's car and cash was definitely a mistake. But an even bigger mistake was picking up a female hitchhiker.

Detour (1946): Several twists of fate place an ordinary man (Tom Neal) in an
inextricable situation which culminates in his strangling a hitchhiker (Ann Savage).

*At a gas station, Al Roberts (Tom Neal) picks up Vera
(Ann Savage). She looks asleep, but suddenly speaks.*
Vera: Where did you leave his body? Where did you
leave the owner of this car? You're not fooling anyone.
This buggy belongs to a guy named Haskell. That's not
you, mister. It just so happens I rode with Charlie
Haskell. All the way from Shreveport.

EDGAR G. ULMER: *DETOUR* (1946)

MARTIN SCORSESE *Detour* was shot in six days
for only $20,000. Ulmer could only rely on his
resourcefulness. In fact, his idiosyncratic style
grew out of such drastic limitations. This is why
he has become such an inspiration over the years
to low-budget filmmakers.

When a second, outrageous twist of fate
crushed Tom Neal, leaving him a murderer, Ulmer
couldn't even afford any special effects. He simply

Outrage (1950): Ida Lupino depicts rape, not as a melodrama but as a subdued behavioral study of the victim (Mala Powers) and of evil in an ordinary small town.

Laurie (Peggy Cummins) lures Bart (John Dall) into a spiral of crime and passion. They are driving away after a holdup.

Bart *(driving)*: You can't shoot a man just because he hesitates.

Laurie *(in glasses and a black beret)*: Maybe not, but you can sure scare them off, like that hotel clerk.

Bart: No, Laurie, I, I . . .

Laurie: You know something . . .

Bart: What?

Laurie *(putting her arm under his)*: I love you. I love you more than anything else in the world . . .

(Later, after another bank holdup, Bart stops her from gunning down a manager in the street. They make their getaway with a police car in hot pursuit.)

Bart *(looking back at the police car, holding a gun)*: You were gonna kill that man.

Laurie *(driving)*: He'd have killed us if he had the chance.

(Bart moves to the back seat as the police car comes closer and closer. He aims his gun, but can't shoot.)

Laurie: Shoot, why don't you shoot? Shoot! Shoot, do you hear me?

Bart *(taking aim again)*: All right.

(He fires at a front tire. The police car careens off the road into a tree.)

Laurie: Get 'em?

Bart *(moving back into his seat, next to her)*: Yeah.

(Laurie's face lights up; she represses a smile.)

JOSEPH H. LEWIS: *GUN CRAZY* (1950)

MARTIN SCORSESE First and foremost, film noir was a style. It combined realism and expressionism, the use of real locations and elaborate shadowplays.

Here the ace cinematographer John Alton deserves a mention. The Hungarian-born master "painted with light" (this was the title of his 1949 textbook, which we were still using as students in the sixties): extreme black and white contrasts, isolated sources of lighting, ominous camera placement, deep perspective . . . The most striking examples of Alton's work are found in Anthony Mann's early films, such as *T-Men* (page 118) and *Raw Deal*.

These were small B-productions where Alton was free to experiment and often took unusual risks. His chiaroscuros alone conjured up the noir mood. "There is no doubt in my mind that the prettiest music is sad," he remarked. "And the most beautiful photography is in a low key, with rich blacks."

Dennis O'Brien (Dennis O'Keefe), an undercover agent investigating a counterfeiting ring, cannot betray his emotions when gangster Moxie (Charles McGraw) decides to execute O'Brien's friend and partner Tony Genaro (Alfred Ryder) who has been caught redhanded.

Moxie *(to Tony)*: Busy little man, eh, snooper?

(Behind him, in the background, we see O'Brien and the rest of the gang entering the dark room.)

Tony *(sweating)*: Almost had you. All of you.

O'Brien *(in close-up)*: Tony . . .

Tony *(in close-up)*: And you, Dennis. So smart. Top-drawer crook. Lived with me and never caught on.

(O'Brien's face registers as he takes the hint about the top drawer.) Top-drawer crook. Always so sharp, always knew all the angles.

(Moxie guns Tony down off-screen. The shot is heard over O'Brien's face.)

Tony *(whispering off-screen before collapsing)*: Sucker.

(As O'Brien lowers his head, the brim of his hat shades his eyes.)

ANTHONY MANN: *T-MEN* (1948)

T-Men (1948): Cinematographer John Alton, more than anyone, created the look of the film noir by "painting with light." Here Dennis O'Keefe is grilling Wallace Ford about the counterfeiters.

MARTIN SCORSESE The paranoia of film noir reached its high point in Robert Aldrich's *Kiss Me Deadly*. Out of the dark, a haunted woman appears to private eye Mike Hammer. She is running away from a mental institution and an unbearable secret. She is not mad though, merely innocent. Destined to be a sacrificial lamb.

SCENE: **RESURRECTION**

Mike Hammer (Ralph Meeker) lies unconscious, while Christina (Cloris Leachman) is being tortured. Only her naked legs are visible. When her screams stop, Dr.

Soberin's (Albert Dekker) voice is heard off-screen:
Dr. Soberin's voice: She passed out.
Gangster's voice: I'll bring her to.
Dr. Soberin's voice: If you revive her, do you know what that would be? Resurrection, that's what it would be. And do you know what resurrection means? It means raise the dead. And just who do you think you are that you think you can raise the dead?
(Hammer regains consciousness. From the floor, all he sees are Christina's naked legs and the pair of pliers held by one of the gangsters.)
ROBERT ALDRICH: *KISS ME DEADLY* (1955)

Kiss Me Deadly (1955): Gaby Rodgers opening Pandora's (radioactive) box at the end of Aldrich's movie, the apogee of film noir paranoia.

Bigger Than Life (1956): Ray probes every aspect of American morality when James Mason (with Christopher Olsen and Barbara Rush) goes mad under the influence of cortisone (then an experimental drug).

5

THE DIRECTOR

AS ICONOCLAST

Frank Sinatra in Otto Preminger's *The Man with the Golden Arm*.

Broken Blossoms (1919): Richard Barthelmess plays a young Chinese man who has lost his Buddhist faith in the slums of London.

SCENE: **TEENAGE HOBOES**

In an open box car, a runaway girl, Sally (Dorothy Coonan), tells her story to two young hoboes, Eddie (Frankie Darro) and Tommy (Edwin Phillips), who are riding the rails across the country.

Sally: So I had to get to my aunt's in Chicago some way. And this is the only way I can do it.

Eddie: Well, don't your folks mind?

Sally: My mother's dead. And we got a big family. With me gone, it means just one less mouth to feed. That's why they were kinda glad to see me go.

WILLIAM WELLMAN: *WILD BOYS OF THE ROAD* (1933)

MARTIN SCORSESE At the opposite end of the spectrum, you found a different breed of iconoclasts: baroque stylists such as Josef von Sternberg. Like Stroheim, Sternberg demanded total control over all aspects of his productions. But his was a voluptuous, dreamlike, supremely artificial world, lovingly composed on the Paramount sound stages. Sternberg's radical stylization proved as provocative as Stroheim's extreme realism. Each film became a ceremonial, with the director orchestrating the most elaborate erotic rituals around his star, Marlene Dietrich.

SCENE: **SEXUAL POLITICS**

Catherine (Marlene Dietrich) surrenders to the most handsome and powerful man of the court, Count Alexei (John Lodge).

Catherine: The woman you adore is quite close to you, isn't she?

Alexei: Catherine, I worship you.

(As he embraces her passionately, they are partially hidden by the bed's thin lace curtain. We see Catherine's hand grab the lace. Preparing for the night, Alexei blows one of the candles. Catherine lies down, but he is not the one on her mind.)

Catherine: Behind the mirror, as you know, there is a flight of stairs. Down below, someone is waiting to come up. Would His Excellency be kind enough to open the door for him carefully so that he can sneak in? *(Obediently, Alexei blows out the remaining candles and slowly exits. His jealousy seems to be reflected by the statue against which he is framed: the tortured figure of Saint Sebastian.)*

JOSEF VON STERNBERG: *THE SCARLET EMPRESS* (1934)

MARTIN SCORSESE Of the seven films Sternberg made with Dietrich, *The Scarlet Empress* was the most baroque and the boldest in its depiction of erotic manipulation as it traced the transformation of an innocent Prussian princess into Catherine the Great, the Empress of Russia. As the heroine quickly discovered, political power and sexual power were inseparable. Her battles were waged in the bedroom, as she learnt the art of choosing and changing lovers at the right time. Catherine showed such considerable skills that she even challenged traditional sexual roles.

Nothing escaped Sternberg's artistic control. He wrote the script, conceived the lighting, composed some of the music, directed the Los Angeles Symphony Orchestra, helped design the sets and sculptures, and probably selected every icon himself. He even claimed that Marlene was just another tool: "Remember that Marlene is not Marlene. I'm Marlene, she knows that better than anyone." To the artist, insisted Sternberg, the subject is incidental and only his vision matters. As he put it: "The camera is a diabolical instrument that conveys ideas with lightning speed. Each picture transliterates a thousand words."

Perhaps the greatest iconoclast of them all was also the youngest: Orson Welles. He was 25 when he landed in Hollywood. In the wake of his radio show, *War of the Worlds*, the young prodigy was given unprecedented latitude by

144

The Scarlet Empress (1934): Marlene Dietrich in Josef von Sternberg's baroque
ale about Catherine the Great's sexual manipulation of political power

Citizen Kane (1941): Orson Welles moved his camera in startling ways to create this revolutionary film.

Kane: . . . the downright villainy of Boss Jim W. Gettys' political machine now in complete control . . .
(Camera dollies up toward Kane in a straight, irresistible movement across the convention floor.)
Kane: I made no campaign promises. Because until a few weeks ago, I had no hope of being elected.
(Crowd laughs and applauds.)
Kane: Now, however, I have something more than a hope. And Jim Gettys . . . Jim Gettys has something less than a chance!
(Tremendous applause. On the balcony, we recognize Leland played by Joseph Cotten. In a box, we see Emily, played by Ruth Warrick, and her son, Junior. She motions, he sits down by her. More applause is heard. In another box, Gettys, played by Ray Collins, is looking down at Kane. A roar from the crowd is heard. A disgusted Gettys puts on his hat and exits.)
ORSON WELLES: *CITIZEN KANE* (1941)

MARTIN SCORSESE Welles was like a young magician enchanted by his own magic. In fact, the most revolutionary aspect of *Citizen Kane* was its self-consciousness. The style drew attention to itself. This contradicted the classical ideal of the invisible camera and seamless cuts. Welles used every narrative technique and filmic device: deep focus, high and low angles, wide angle lenses. "I want to use the motion picture camera as an instrument of poetry," he said. And somehow Welles's passion for the medium became the great excitement of the piece itself.

ORSON WELLES (1970) You see, I had the best contract anybody has ever had for *Kane*. Nobody comes on the set. Nobody gets to look at the rushes. Nothing! You just make the picture and that's it. If I hadn't had that contract, they would have stopped me at the beginning just by the nature of the script. But it was such conditions!

RKO, including what is known today as the right to final cut. At the time, only Charlie Chaplin had such creative control over his productions.

For his first film, Welles set out to explore the many facets of media baron William Randolph Hearst, whose abuse of wealth and power defied America's democratic traditions. Some in Hollywood were so incensed that they put pressure on RKO to destroy the negative. Fortunately, they didn't succeed.

SCENE: **ENCHANTED BY HIS OWN MAGIC**
At Madison Square Garden, under his own banner, Kane attacks political boss Jim Gettys.

The Magnificent Ambersons (1942): Welles lost control over this film (above, Tim Holt and Dolores Costello), which was edited and changed by the studio without his consent.

I've never had anything remotely equal to that contract since. So it isn't just the success. What spoiled me is having had the joy of that kind of liberty once in my life and never having been able to enjoy it again.

MARTIN SCORSESE Orson Welles inspired more would-be directors than any other filmmaker since D. W. Griffith. Yet Welles didn't change the status of the Hollywood director. He actually lost all his privileges a year after *Citizen Kane* on *The Magnificent Ambersons*, which was chopped down and even partially reshot in his absence.

ORSON WELLES (1970) Do you know that I always liked Hollywood very much? It just wasn't reciprocated.

MARTIN SCORSESE Throughout his career, Welles pushed the creative envelope in so many ways. To trace Kane's political ambitions, for instance, he created fake newsreel footage. And to give it the appropriate look, he had editor Robert Wise drag the film across a concrete floor. This was an opportunity for Welles to recall William Randolph Hearst's fondness for dictators: you saw Kane posing with Hitler for the photographers.

At the same time, in his first talking picture, Charlie Chaplin dared to aim at the fascist powers directly. At the risk of infuriating America's isolationist forces, he took on the dictators singlehandedly. A comedy drawing on such topical horrors as racial persecutions and concentration camps, *The Great Dictator* presented Chaplin with another major challenge: he gave himself a double role, that of the monster, dictator Hynkel and the victim, the Jewish barber.

Of course, even the renegades like Charlie Chaplin and Orson Welles had to work around the censors. The content of American films was still strictly controlled. Adult themes and images were too often curtailed or suppressed. But after World War II, audiences wanted pictures to be truer to life. A few of our filmmakers started challenging the rules. Elia Kazan led the assault against the censors. His *Streetcar Named Desire* caused the first major breach in Hollywood's Production Code.

Kazan fought tooth and nail, frame by frame, to preserve the integrity of Tennessee Williams's drama when he adapted it to the screen. This meant exposing the overtly carnal desires of Stanley and his battered, pregnant wife, Stella. However, several close shots of Kim Hunter could not be included in the film as it was originally released, because the Legion of Decency objected to their sensuality. The studio decided to cut them and replaced the jazz score with more conventional music.

ELIA KAZAN (1981) The camera is more than a recorder, it's a microscope. It penetrates, it goes into people and you see their most private and concealed thoughts. I have been able to do that with actors. I have revealed things that actors didn't even know they were revealing about themselves.

SCENE: **CONCEALED THOUGHTS**

In a park Terry Malloy (Marlon Brando) courts Edie Doyle (Eva Marie Saint). He is wearing one of her gloves, which he picked up earlier when she dropped it.
Terry: You know, I've seen you a lot of times before. Remember, parochial school down at Paluski Street. Seven, eight years ago, your hair, you had your hair…
Edie: Braids.
Terry: Looked like a hunk of rope. You had wires on your teeth and glasses, everything . . . *(He puts a chewing gum into his mouth.)* You was really a mess. *(She reacts and removes her glove from his hand.)*
Terry: Aw, don't get sore, I was just kiddin' you a little bit. I just mean to tell ya that you grew up very nice.
ELIA KAZAN: *ON THE WATERFRONT* (1954)

MARTIN SCORSESE I was 12 years old when I saw *On the Waterfront*. It was a breakthrough for me. Kazan was forging a new acting style. It had the appearance of realism. But actually it revealed something in the natural behavior of people that I hadn't seen on the screen before: the truth behind the posture. "Brando," Kazan observed, "was the only actor I can describe as a genius. He had that ambivalence that I believe is essential in depicting humanity, both strength and sensibility."

SCENE: **THE TRUTH BEHIND THE POSTURE**

Terry (Marlon Brando) knocks on the door of Edie's apartment (Eva Marie Saint).

But he couldn't stand being an "[...] studio projects and moved to Lo[...] *Lolita*. He stayed there and has [...] Hollywood since. He is one of t[...] clasts who has enjoyed the luxur[...] completely on his own terms.

THE DECISIVE FACTOR

Charlotte Haze (Shelley Winters) g[...]
house to Professor Humbert F[...]
Mason), a distinguished-looking [...]
for a room to rent.

Charlotte: Uh, back here, we have t[...]
where we have our informal meals.

Humbert: Perhaps, if you would . .

Charlotte: My pastries win prizes a[...]

Humbert: Perhaps, if you would [...]
phone number. That would give me [...]
over.

(Charlotte leads Humbert toward t[...]

Charlotte: Oh, you must see the gar[...]
You must!

(Lolita, played by Sue Lyon, is in a[...]
sun, listening to loud popular musi[...]

Charlotte *(off-screen)*: My flowers[...]
here. They're the talk of the neighb[...]

Charlotte: Voilà!

(Humbert is hypnotized by Lolit[...]
him with an enigmatic smile.)

Charlotte's voice (off-screen): M[...]
uh, oh, my daughter. Uh, darlin[...]
please. I can offer you a comfort[...]
garden, a congenial atmosphere, n[...]

(Lolita removes her dark glasses t[...]
at the professor.)

Humbert: We haven't discussed u[...]

Charlotte: Oh, something nomina[...]
hundred a month.

Humbert: Yes, that's very, uh . . .

A Streetcar Named Desire (1951): Kazan fought vigorously against the censors to keep the sensual scenes of Marlon Brando and Kim Hunter.

Bonnie and Clyde (1967): Penn's movie (starring F
graphic depiction of violence, was one of the final ass

Lolita (1962): Kubrick defiantly dramatizes a forbidden subject: the infatuation of a middle-aged man (James Mason) for a sexually-precocious minor (Sue Lyon).

Cat People

(JACQUES TOURNEUR, 1942)

Sc.: DeWitt Bodeen, from a story by Bodeen and Val Lewton. *Ph.:* Nicholas Musuraca. *Mus.:* Roy Webb. *Ed.:* Mark Robson. *Prod.:* Val Lewton. (RKO). *Cast:* Simone Simon, Kent Smith, Tom Conway, Jane Randolph, Jack Holt, Alan Napier, Elizabeth Russell, Elizabeth Dunne. *VHS, LD* *

Citizen Kane

(ORSON WELLES, 1941)

Sc.: Herman J. Mankiewicz, Orson Welles. *Ph.:* Gregg Toland. *Mus.:* Bernard Herrmann. *Ed.:* Robert Wise. *Prod.:* Orson Welles for Mercury Productions. (RKO). *Cast:* Orson Welles, Joseph Cotten, Everett Sloane, Dorothy Comingore, Ray Collins, William Alland, Agnes Moorehead, Ruth Warrick, Paul Stewart. *VHS, LD*

Colorado Territory

(RAOUL WALSH, 1949)

Sc.: John Twist, Edmund H. North, from the novel *High Sierra* by W.R. Burnett. *Ph.:* Sid Hickox. *Mus.:* David Buttolph. *Prod.:* Anthony Veiller. (Warner Bros.). *Cast.:* Joel McCrea, Virginia Mayo, Dorothy Malone, Henry Hull, John Archer, James Mitchell, Morris Ankrum. *

Crime Wave

(ANDRÉ DE TOTH, 1954)

Sc.: Crane Wilbur, adapted by Bernard Gordon, Richard Wormser, from the *Saturday Evening Post* story "Criminal Mark" by John and Ward Hawkins. *Ph.:* Bert Glennon. *Mus.:* David Buttolph. *Prod.:* Bryan Foy. (Warner Bros.). *Cast:* Gene Nelson, Phyllis Kirk, Sterling Hayden, James Bell, Ted De Corsia, Charles Buchinsky, Ned Young, Jay Novello. *

The Crowd

(KING VIDOR, 1928)

Sc.: King Vidor, John V. A. Weaver, Harry Behn, from a story by King Vidor. *Titles:* Joseph Farnham. *Ph.:* Henry Sharp. *Prod.:* King Vidor. (MGM). *Cast:* Eleanor Boardman, James Murray, Bert Roach, Estelle Clark. *VHS, LD* *

Death's Marathon

(D. W. GRIFFITH, 1913).

Sc.: W. E. Wing. *Ph.:* Billy Bitzer. *Prod.:* Biograph. *Cast:* Blanche Sweet, Henry B. Walthall, Robert Harron, Lionel Barrymore, Alfred Paget. *

Detour

(EDGAR G. ULMER, 1946)

Sc.: Martin Goldsmith. *Ph.:* Benjamin H. Kline. *Mus.:* Leo Erdody. *Prod.:* Leon Fromkess. (PRC). *Cast:* Tom Neal, Ann Savage, Claudia Drake, Edmund MacDonald. *VHS*

Double Indemnity

(BILLY WILDER, 1944).

Sc.: Raymond Chandler, Billy Wilder, from the novel by James M. Cain. *Ph.:* John F. Seitz. *Mus.:* Miklos Rosza. *Prod.:* Buddy DeSylva, Joseph Sistrom. (Paramount). *Cast:* Fred MacMurray, Barbara Stanwyck, Edward G. Robinson, Porter Hall, Jean Heather, Tom Powers. *VHS, LD* *

Duel in the Sun

(KING VIDOR AND UNCREDITED DIRECTOR WILLIAM DIETERLE, 1946).

Sc.: David O. Selznick, from the novel by Niven Busch. *Adapt.:* Oliver H. P. Garrett. *Vis. cons.:* Josef von Sternberg. *Ph.:* Lee Garmes, Hal Rosson, Ray Rennahan (Technicolor). *Mus.:* Dimitri Tiomkin. *Prod.:* David O. Selznick for Vanguard. (S.R.O.) *Cast:* Jennifer Jones, Joseph Cotten, Gregory Peck, Lionel Barrymore, Lillian Gish, Walter Huston, Herbert Marshall, Charles Bickford, Tilly Losch, Harry Carey, and the voice of Orson Welles. *VHS*

East of Eden

(ELIA KAZAN, 1955)

Sc.: Paul Osborn, from the novel by John Steinbeck. *Ph.:* Ted McCord (Warnercolor, CinemaScope). *Mus.:* Leonard Rosenman. *Prod.:* Elia Kazan. (Warner Bros.). *Cast:* James Dean, Julie Harris, Raymond Massey, Richard Davalos, Burl Ives, Jo Van Fleet, Albert Dekker, Lois Smith, Timothy Carey, Nick Dennis. *VHS*

Faces

(JOHN CASSAVETES, 1968)

Sc.: John Cassavetes. *Ph.:* Al Ruban. *Mus.:* Jack Ackerman. *Prod.:* Maurice McEndree. *Cast:* Gena Rowlands, John Marley, Lynn Carlin, Seymour Cassel, Fred Draper, Val Avery, Dorothy Gulliver, Joanne Moore Jordan, Darlene Conley. *VHS*

The Fall of the Roman Empire

(ANTHONY MANN, 1964)

Sc.: Ben Barzman, Basilio Franchina, Philip Yordan. *Ph.:* Robert Krasker (Technicolor, Ultra Panavision 70). *Mus.:* Dimitri Tiomkin. *2nd unit dir.:* Andrew Marton, Yakima Canutt. *Prod.:* Samuel Bronston, Michael Waszynski, Jaime Prades for Samuel Bronston Productions. *Cast:* Sophia Loren, Stephen Boyd, Alec Guinness, James Mason, Christopher Plummer, Anthony Quayle, John Ireland, Mel Ferrer, Omar Sharif, Eric Porter, Douglas Wilmer, Finlay Currie. *VHS, LD*

Footlight Parade

(LLOYD BACON, 1933)

Sc.: Manuel Seff, James Seymour. *Ph.:* George Barnes. *Mus.:* Harry Warren, Sammy Fain. *Lyr.:* Al Dubin, Irving Kahal. *Chor.:* Busby Berkeley. *Prod.:* Darryl Zanuck, Robert Lord. (Warner Bros.). *Cast:* James Cagney, Joan Blondell, Ruby Keeler, Dick Powell, Guy Kibbee, Frank McHugh. *VHS, LD*

Force of Evil

(ABRAHAM POLONSKY, 1948)

Sc.: Abraham Polonsky, Ira Wolfert, from the novel *Tucker's People* by Ira Wolfert. *Ph.:* George Barnes. *Mus.:* David Raksin. *Dial. dir.:* Don Weis. *Asst. dir.:* Robert Aldrich. *Prod.:* Bob Roberts for Enterprise Studio. (MGM). *Cast:* John Garfield, Beatrice Pearson, Thomas Gomez, Marie Windsor, Roy Roberts, Howland Chamberlain, Sheldon Leonard. *VHS, LD* *

42nd Street

(LLOYD BACON, 1933)

Sc.: James Seymour, Rian James, from the novel by Bradford Ropes. *Ph.:* Sol Polito. *Mus.:* Harry Warren. *Lyr.:* Al Dubin. *Chor.:* Busby Berkeley. *Prod.:* Darryl F. Zanuck, Hal B. Wallis. (Warner Bros.). *Cast:* Warner Baxter, Bebe Daniels, George Brent, Ruby Keeler, Dick Powell, Ginger Rogers, Una Merkel, Guy Kibbee, Ned Sparks. *VHS, LD*

Forty Guns

(SAMUEL FULLER, 1957)

Sc.: Samuel Fuller. *Ph.:* Joseph Biroc (CinemaScope). *Mus.:* Harry Sukman. *Prod.:* Samuel Fuller for Globe Enterprises. (20th Century-Fox). *Cast:* Barbara Stanwyck, Barry Sullivan, Dean Jagger, John Ericson, Gene Barry, Robert Dix, Hank Worden. *

The Furies

(ANTHONY MANN, 1950)

Sc.: Charles Schnee, from a story by Niven Busch. *Ph.:* Victor Milner. *Mus.:* Franz Waxman. *Prod.:* Hal B. Wallis. (Paramount). *Cast:* Barbara Stanwyck, Wendell Corey, Walter Huston, Judith Anderson, Gilbert Roland, Thomas Gomez, Beulah Bondi, Albert Dekker, Wallace Ford, Blanche Yurka, Frank Ferguson. *

Gold Diggers of 1933

(MERVYN LEROY, 1933).

Sc.: Erwin Gelsey, James Seymour, from the Broadway play *The Gold Diggers* by Avery Hopwood. *Dial.:* David Boehm, Ben Markson. *Ph.:* Sol Polito. *Mus.:* Harry Warren. *Lyrics:* Al Dubin. *Chor.:* Busby Berkeley. *Prod.:* Robert Lord. (Warner Bros.). Cast: Warren William, Joan Blondell, Aline MacMahon, Ruby Keeler, Dick Powell, Ginger Rogers, Ned Sparks, Guy Kibbee. *VHS, LD* *

The Great Dictator

(CHARLES CHAPLIN, 1940)

Sc.: Charles Chaplin. *Ph.:* Karl Struss, Rollie Totheroh. *Mus.:* Charles Chaplin, Meredith Wilson. *Prod.:* Charles Chaplin. *Cast:* Charles Chaplin, Paulette Goddard, Jack Oakie, Reginald Gardiner, Henry Daniell, Billy Gilbert, Lucien Prival. *VHS*

The Great Train Robbery

(EDWIN S. PORTER, 1903)

Sc.: Edwin S. Porter. *Prod.:* The Edison Company. *Cast:* George Barnes, A. C. Abadie, Marie Murray, G. M. Anderson. *VHS, LD* *

Gun Crazy

(JOSEPH H. LEWIS, 1950)

Sc.: MacKinlay Kantor, Dalton Trumbo, from a *Saturday Evening Post* story by Kantor. *Ph.:* Russell Harlan. *Mus.:* Victor Young. *Prod.:* Frank and Maurice King for King Brothers. (United Artists). *Cast:* John Dall, Peggy Cummins, Berry Kroeger, Annabel Shaw, Morris Carnovsky, Nedrick Young. *VHS* *

Hell's Highway

(ROWLAND BROWN, 1932)

Sc.: Rowland Brown, Samuel Ornitz, Robert Tasker. *Ph.:* Edward Cronjager. *Mus.:* Max Steiner. *Prod.:* David O. Selznick. (RKO). *Cast:* Richard Dix, Tom Brown, Rochelle Hudson, Louise Carter, C. Henry Gordon, Oscar Apfel, Warner Richmond, Charles Middleton, John Arledge, Clarence Muse. *

Her Man

(TAY GARNETT, 1930)

Sc.: Tom Buckingham, from a story by Tay Garnett, Howard Higgin. *Ph.:* Edward Snyder. *Mus.:* Josiah Zuro. *Prod.:* E. B. Derr, Tay Garnett. (Pathé Exchange). *Cast:* Helen Twelvetrees, Marjorie Rambeau, Ricardo Cortez, Phillips Holmes, James Gleason, Harry Sweet, Franklin Pangborn, Slim Summerville. *

High Sierra

(RAOUL WALSH, 1941)

Sc.: John Huston, W. R. Burnett, from the novel by W. R. Burnett. *Ph.:* Tony Gaudio. *Mus.:* Adolph Deutsch. *Prod.:* Hal B. Wallis, Mark Hellinger. (Warner Bros.). *Cast:* Humphrey Bogart, Ida Lupino, Alan Curtis, Arthur Kennedy, Joan Leslie, Henry Hull, Henry Travers, Elizabeth Risdon, Cornel Wilde. *VHS, LD* *

Intolerance

(D. W. GRIFFITH, 1916)

Sc.: D. W. Griffith. *Ph.:* Billy Bitzer. *Cam.:* Karl Brown. *Mus.:* D. W. Griffith, Joseph Carl Breil. *Asst. dir.:* Allan Dwan, Erich von Stroheim, W. S. Van Dyke, Tod Browning, Jack Conway, George Hill, Victor Fleming. *Prod.:* D. W. Griffith for Wark Producing Corporation. *Cast:* Lillian Gish, Mae Marsh, Constance Talmadge, Margery Wilson, Robert Harron, Miriam Cooper, Walter Long, Howard Gaye, Bessie Love, George Walsh, Eugene Pallette, Elmer Clifton, Alfred Paget, Seena Owen, Tully Marshall. *VHS, LD*

I Walk Alone

(BYRON HASKIN, 1948)

Sc.: Charles Schnee, adapted by Robert Smith, John Bright, from the play *Beggars Are Coming to Town* by Theodore Reeves. *Ph.:* Leo Tover. *Mus.:* Victor Young. *Prod.:* Hal B. Wallis. (Paramount). *Cast:* Burt Lancaster, Lizabeth Scott, Kirk Douglas, Wendell Corey, George Rigaud, Marc Lawrence, Mike Mazurski. *

I Walked with a Zombie

(JACQUES TOURNEUR, 1943)

Sc.: Curt Siodmak, Ardel Wray, from an *American Weekly* story by Inez Wallace. *Ph.:* J. Roy Hunt. *Mus.:* Roy Webb. *Ed.:* Mark Robson. *Prod.:* Val Lewton. (RKO). *Cast:* Frances Dee, James Ellison, Tom Conway, Edith Barrett, Christine Gordon, James Bell, Teresa Harris, Darby Jones, Sir Lancelot. *VHS, LD* *

Johnny Guitar

(NICHOLAS RAY, 1954)

Sc.: Philip Yordan, from the novel by Roy Chanslor. *Ph.:* Harry Stradling (Trucolor). *Mus.:* Victor Young. *Prod.:* Herbert J. Yates. (Republic Pictures). *Cast:* Joan Crawford, Sterling Hayden, Mercedes McCambridge, Scott Brady, Ward Bond, Ben Cooper, Ernest Borgnine, John Carradine, Royal Dano, Frank Ferguson. *VHS* *

Kiss Me Deadly

(ROBERT ALDRICH, 1955)

Sc.: A. I. Bezzerides, from the novel by Mickey Spillane. *Ph.:* Ernest Laszlo. *Mus.:* Frank DeVol. *Prod.:* Robert Aldrich, Victor Saville for Parklane Productions. (United Artists). *Cast:* Ralph Meeker, Marion Carr, Albert Dekker, Paul Stewart, Maxine Cooper, Gaby Rodgers, Wesley Addy, Nick Dennis, Cloris Leachman, Jack Lambert, Jack Elam. *VHS, LD* *

Land of the Pharaohs

(HOWARD HAWKS, 1955)

Sc.: William Faulkner, Harry Kurnitz, Harold Jack Bloom. *Ph.:* Lee Garmes, Russell Harlan (Warnercolor, CinemaScope). *Mus.:* Dimitri Tiomkin. *2nd unit dir.:* Noel Howard. *Prod.:* Howard Hawks for Continental Productions. (Warner Bros.). *Cast:* Jack Hawkins, Joan Collins, Dewey Martin, Alexis Minotis, James Robertson Justice, Luisa Boni, Sydney Chaplin. *VHS, LD* *

Leave Her to Heaven

(JOHN M. STAHL, 1945)

Sc.: Jo Swerling, from the novel by Ben Ames Williams. *Ph.:* Leon Shamroy (Technicolor). *Mus.:* Alfred Newman. *Prod.:* William A. Bacher. (20th Century-Fox). *Cast:* Gene Tierney, Cornel Wilde, Jeanne Crain, Vincent Price, Mary Philips, Ray Collins, Gene Lockhart, Darryl Hickman, Chill Wills. *VHS, LD* *

The Left-Handed Gun

(ARTHUR PENN, 1958)

Sc.: Leslie Stevens, from the teleplay *The Death of Billy the Kid* by Gore Vidal. *Ph.:* J. Peverell Marley. *Mus.:* Alexander Courage. *Prod.:* Fred Coe. (Warner Bros.). *Cast:* Paul Newman, Lita Milan, John Dehner, Hurd Hatfield, James Best. *VHS*

Letter from an Unknown Woman

(MAX OPHULS, 1948)

Sc.: Howard Koch, Max Ophuls, from the novella by Stefan Zweig. *Ph.:* Franz Planer. *Mus.:* Daniele Amfitheatrof. *Prod.:* John Houseman. (Universal-International). *Cast:* Joan Fontaine, Louis Jourdan, Mady Christians, Marcel Journet, John Good, Carol Yorke, Art Smith. *VHS, LD* *

Lolita

(STANLEY KUBRICK, 1962)

Sc.: Vladimir Nabokov, from his novel. *Ph.:* Oswald Morris. *Mus.:* Nelson Riddle. *Prod.:* James B. Harris for Seven Arts-Anya-Transworld. (MGM). *Cast:* James Mason, Shelley Winters, Peter Sellers, Sue Lyon, Marianne Stone, Diana Decker. *VHS, LD* *

The Magnificent Ambersons

(ORSON WELLES, 1942)

Sc.: Orson Welles, from the novel by Booth Tarkington (additional contributions by Jack Moss, Joseph Cotten). *Ph.:* Stanley Cortez. *Mus.:* Bernard Herrman, Roy Webb. *Ed.:* Robert Wise. (Additional scenes filmed by Freddie Fleck, Robert Wise, Jack Moss). *Prod.:* Orson Welles for Mercury Productions. (RKO). Cast: Tim Holt, Joseph Cotten, Dolores Costello, Agnes Moorehead, Anne Baxter, Ray Collins, Richard Bennett. *VHS, LD* *

The Man with the Golden Arm

(OTTO PREMINGER, 1955)

Sc.: Walter Newman, Lewis Meltzer, from the novel by Nelson Algren. *Ph.:* Sam Leavitt. *Mus.:* Elmer Bernstein. *Titl.:* Saul Bass. *Prod.:* Otto Preminger for Carlyle Productions. (United Artists). *Cast:* Frank Sinatra, Kim Novak, Eleanor Parker, Arnold Stang, Darren McGavin, Robert Strauss, George Matthews, John Conte, Doro Merande, George E. Stone, Emile Meyer. *VHS*

Meet Me in St. Louis

(VINCENTE MINNELLI, 1944)

Sc.: Irving Bretcher, Fred F. Finklehoffe, from *The New Yorker* stories and novel by Sally Benson. *Ph.:* George Folsey (Technicolor). *Mus.:* Hugh Martin, Ralph Blane. *Orch.:* Roger Edens, Conrad Salinger. *Chor.:* Charles Walters. *Prod.:* Arthur Freed. (MGM). *Cast:* Judy Garland, Margaret O'Brien, Mary Astor, Lucille Bremer, Leon Ames, Tom Drake, Marjorie Main. *VHS, LD*

Murder by Contract

(IRVING LERNER, 1958)

Sc.: Ben Simcoe. *Ph.:* Lucien Ballard. *Mus.:* Perry Botkin. *Prod.:* Leon Chooluck for Orbit Productions. (Columbia). *Cast:* Vince Edwards, Philip Pine, Herschel Bernardi, Caprice Toriel, Michael Granger. *

The Musketeers of Pig Alley

(D. W. GRIFFITH, 1912)

Sc.: D. W. Griffith. *Ph.:* Billy Bitzer. *Prod.:* Biograph. *Cast:* Elmer Booth, Alfred Paget, Lillian Gish, Walter C. Miller, Lionel Barrymore, Harry Carey, Robert Harron, Dorothy Gish. *VHS* *

My Dream is Yours

(MICHAEL CURTIZ, 1949)

Sc.: Harry Kurnitz, Dane Lurrier, from a story by Jerry Wald. *Ph.:* Ernest Haller (Technicolor). *Mus.:* Harry Warren, Ralph Blane. *Prod.:* Michael Curtiz. (Warner Bros.). *Cast:* Doris Day, Jack Carson, Lee Bowman, Adolphe Menjou, Eve Arden, S.Z. Sakall, Edgar Kennedy, Sheldon Leonard. *VHS, LD* *

The Naked Kiss

(SAMUEL FULLER, 1964)

Sc.: Samuel Fuller. *Ph.:* Stanley Cortez. *Mus.:* Paul Dunlap. *Prod.:* Samuel Fuller for Leon Fromkess–Sam Firks Productions. (Allied Artists). *Cast:* Constance Towers, Anthony Eisley, Michael Dante, Virginia Grey, Patsy Kelly. *VHS, LD*

The Naked Spur

(ANTHONY MANN, 1953).

Sc.: Sam Rolfe, Harold Jack Bloom. *Ph.:* William Mellor (Technicolor). *Mus.:* Bronislau Kaper. *Prod.:* William W. Wright. (MGM). *Cast:* James Stewart, Janet Leigh, Robert Ryan, Ralph Meeker, Millard Mitchell. *VHS, LD*

One, Two, Three

(BILLY WILDER, 1961)

Sc.: Billy Wilder, I. A. L. Diamond, from the play by Ferenc Molnar. *Ph.:* Daniel Fapp (Panavision). *Prod.:* Billy Wilder for Mirisch Company–Pyramid. (United Artists). *Cast:* James Cagney, Horst Buchholz, Pamela Tiffin, Arlene Francis, Lilo Pulver, Howard St. John, Hanns Lothar, Leon Askin, Peter Capell, Red Buttons. *VHS* *

On the Waterfront

(ELIA KAZAN, 1954)

Sc.: Budd Schulberg, from his original story based on a series of articles by Malcolm Johnson. *Ph.:* Boris Kaufman. *Mus.:* Leonard Bernstein. *Prod.:* Sam Spiegel for Horizon Films. (Columbia). *Cast:* Marlon Brando, Eva Marie Saint, Karl Malden, Lee J. Cobb, Rod Steiger, Pat Henning, James Westerfield, Leif Ericson. *VHS, LD*

Outrage

(IDA LUPINO, 1950)

Sc.: Collier Young, Malvin Wald, Ida Lupino. *Ph.:* Archie Stout. *Mus.:* Paul Sawtell. *Prod. des.:* Harry Horner. *Prod.:* Collier Young for Filmakers. (RKO). Cast: Mala Powers, Tod Andrews, Robert Clarke, Raymond Bond, Lilian Hamilton, Rita Lupino, Jerry Paris. *

The Phenix City Story

(PHIL KARLSON, 1955)

Sc.: Crane Wilbur, Daniel Mainwaring. *Ph.:* Harry Neumann. *Mus.:* Harry Sukman. *Prod.:* Samuel Bischoff, David Diamond. (Allied Artists). *Cast:* John McIntyre, Richard Kiley, Edward Andrews, Kathryn Grant, James Edwards.

Pickup on South Street

(SAMUEL FULLER, 1953)

Sc.: Samuel Fuller, from a story by Dwight Taylor. *Ph.:* Joe MacDonald. *Mus.:* Leigh Harline. *Prod.:* Jules Schermer (20th Century-Fox). *Cast:* Richard Widmark, Jean Peters, Thelma Ritter, Murvyn Vye, Richard Kiley, Willis Bouchey, George E. Stone. *VHS* *

Point Blank

(JOHN BOORMAN, 1967).

Sc.: Alexander Jacobs, David Newhouse, Rafe Newhouse, from the novel *The Hunter* by Richard Stark (aka Donald Westlake). *Ph.:* Philip H. Lathrop (Metrocolor, Panavision). *Col. cons.:* Bill Stair. *Mus.:* Johnny Mandel. *Ed.:* Henry Berman. *Prod.:* Judd Bernard, Robert Chartoff. (MGM). *Cast:* Lee Marvin, Angie Dickinson, Keenan Wynn, Carroll O'Connor, Michael Strong, John Vernon. *VHS, LD*

The Public Enemy

(WILLIAM WELLMAN, 1931)

Sc.: Kubec Glasmon, John Bright, adapted by Harvey Thew from the story "Beer and Blood" by Bright. *Ph.:* Dev Jennings. *Mus.:* David Mendoza. *Prod.:* Darryl Zanuck, Hal B. Wallis. (Warner Bros.). *Cast:* James Cagney, Jean Harlow, Edward Woods, Joan Blondell, Donald Cook, Mae Clark, Leslie Fenton, Beryl Mercer. *VHS*

Raw Deal

(ANTHONY MANN, 1948)

Sc.: Leopold Atlas, John C. Higgins, from a story by Arnold B. Armstrong and Audrey Ashley. *Ph.:* John Alton. *Mus.:* Paul Sawtell. *Prod.:* Edward Small for Edward Small Productions. (Eagle-Lion). *Cast:* Dennis O'Keefe, Claire Trevor, Marsha Hunt, John Ireland, Raymond Burr. *VHS, LD* *

The Red House

(DELMER DAVES, 1947)

Sc.: Delmer Daves, from the novel by George Agnew Chamberlain. *Ph.:* Bert Glennon. *Mus.:* Miklos Rosza. *Prod.:* Sol Lesser for Thalia Productions. *Cast:* Edward G. Robinson, Lon McCallister, Judith Anderson, Allene Roberts, Julie London, Rory Calhoun, Ona Munson. *VHS* *

The Regeneration

(RAOUL WALSH, 1915)

Sc.: Raoul Walsh, Carl Harbaugh, from a play by Owen Kildare, Walter Hackett. *Ph.:* George Benoit. *Prod.:* William Fox. (Fox Film). *Cast:* Rockliffe Fellowes, Anna Q. Nilsson, William A. Sheer. *VHS* *

The Roaring Twenties

(RAOUL WALSH, 1939)

Sc.: Jerry Wald, Richard Macaulay, Robert Rossen, from a story by Mark Hellinger. *Ph.:* Ernest Haller. *Mus.:* Heinz Roemheld, Ray Heindorf. *Montages:* Don Siegel. *Prod.:* Mark Hellinger, Hal B. Wallis. (Warner Bros.). *Cast:* James Cagney, Priscilla Lane, Humphrey Bogart, Gladys George, Frank McHugh, Paul Kelly, Elizabeth Risdon. *VHS, LD*

The Robe

(HENRY KOSTER, 1953)

Sc.: Philip Dunne, from the novel by Lloyd C. Douglas, adapted by Gina Kaus. *Ph.:* Leon Shamroy (Technicolor, CinemaScope). *Mus.:* Alfred Newman. *Prod.:* Frank Ross. (20th Century-Fox). *Cast:* Richard Burton, Jean Simmons, Victor Mature, Michael Rennie, Jay Robinson, Dean Jagger, Torin Thatcher, Richard Boone, Betta St. John, Jeff Morrow, Ernest Thesiger, Dawn Addams. *VHS, LD*

Samson and Delilah

(CECIL B. DE MILLE, 1949)

Sc.: Jesse Lasky, Jr., Fredric M. Frank, from a story by Harold Lamb and Vladimir Jabotinsky. *Ph.:* George Barnes (Technicolor), Dewey Wrigley. *Mus.:* Victor Young. *Prod.:* Cecil B. De Mille. (Paramount). *Cast:* Hedy Lamarr, Victor Mature, George Sanders, Angela Lansbury, Henry Wilcoxon, Olive Deering, Fay Holden, Julia Faye, Russ Tamblyn, William Farnum. *VHS, LD*

Scarface

(HOWARD HAWKS, 1932)

Sc.: Ben Hecht, Seton I. Miller, John Lee Mahin, W. R. Burnett, Fred Palsey, from the novel by Armitage Trail. *Ph.:* Lee Garmes, L. William O'Connell. *Mus.:* Adolph Tandler, Gus Arnheim. *Prod.:* Howard Hughes, Howard Hawks for Atlantic Pictures. (United Artists). *Cast:* Paul Muni, Ann Dvorak, Karen Morley, Osgood Perkins, Boris Karloff, George Raft, Vince Barnett, C. Henry Gordon, Tully Marshall. *VHS, LD*

The Scarlet Empress

(JOSEF VON STERNBERG, 1934)

Sc.: Josef von Sternberg, from the diary of Catherine the Great, adapted by Manuel Komroff. *Ph.:* Bert Glennon. *Mus.:* W. Franke Harling, John M. Leipold, (and Joseph von Sternberg). *Prod.:* Adolph Zukor. (Paramount). *Cast:* Marlene Dietrich, John Lodge, Sam Jaffe, Louise Dresser, Gavin Gordon, C. Aubrey Smith, Maria Sieber, Ruthelma Stevens. *VHS* *

Scarlet Street

(FRITZ LANG, 1945)

Sc.: Dudley Nichols, from the novel and play *La Chienne* by Georges de la Fouchardiere in collaboration with Mouezy-Eon. *Ph.:* Milton Krasner. *Mus.:* Hans J. Salter. *Prod.:* Fritz Lang, Walter Wanger for Diana Productions. (Universal). *Cast:* Edward G. Robinson, Joan Bennett, Dan Duryea, Jess Barker, Margaret Lindsay, Rosalind Ivan. *VHS*

The Searchers

(JOHN FORD, 1956)

Sc.: Frank S. Nugent, from the novel by Alan LeMay. *Ph.:* Winton C. Hoch (Technicolor, VistaVision). *Mus.:* Max Steiner. *Prod.:* Merian C. Cooper. (Warner Bros.). *Cast:* John Wayne, Jeffrey Hunter, Vera Miles, Ward Bond, Natalie Wood, John Qualen, Olive Carey, Henry Brandon, Ken Curtis, Harry Carey, Jr., Hank Worden, Patrick Wayne. *VHS, LD*

Seventh Heaven

(FRANK BORZAGE, 1927)

Sc.: Benjamin Glazer, from the play by Austin Strong. *Titl.:* Katharine Hilliker, H.H. Caldwell. *Ph.:* Ernest Palmer. *Mus.:* William Perry. *Prod.:* Frank Borzage, Sol M. Wurtzel. (Fox Film). *Cast:* Janet Gaynor, Charles Farrell, Ben Bard, David Butler, Albert Gran, Gladys Brockwell, Emile Chautard, George Stone. *

She Wore a Yellow Ribbon

(JOHN FORD, 1949)

Sc.: Frank S. Nugent, Laurence Stallings, from the story "War Party" by James Warner Bellah. *Ph.:* Winton C. Hoch (Technicolor), Charles P. Boyle (2nd unit). *Mus.:* Richard Hageman. *2nd unit dir.:* Cliff Smith. *Prod.:* John Ford, Merian C. Cooper for Argosy Pictures. (RKO). *Cast:* John Wayne, Joanne Dru, John Agar, Ben Johnson, Harry Carey, Jr., Victor McLaglen. *VHS, LD*

Shock Corridor

(SAMUEL FULLER, 1963)

Sc.: Samuel Fuller, from his script "Straitjacket." *Ph.:* Stanley Cortez. *Mus.:* Paul Dunlap. *Prod.:* Samuel Fuller for Leon Fromkess—Sam Firks Productions. (Allied Artists). *Cast:* Peter Breck, Constance Towers, Gene Evans, James Best, Hari Rhodes, Larry Tucker. *VHS, LD*

Silver Lode

(ALLAN DWAN, 1954)

Sc.: Karen De Wolfe. *Ph.:* John Alton (Technicolor). *Mus.:* Louis Forbes. *Prod.:* Benedict Bogeaus (RKO). *Cast:* John Payne, Dan Duryea, Lizabeth Scott, Dolores Moran, Emile Meyer, Harry Carey, Jr., Morris Ankrum, Robert Warwick, Stuart Whitman. *VHS* *

Howard Hawks

Some Came Running

(VINCENTE MINNELLI, 1958)

Sc.: John Patrick, Arthur Sheekman, from the novel by James Jones. *Ph.:* William H. Daniels (Metrocolor, CinemaScope). *Mus.:* Elmer Bernstein. *Prod.:* Sol C. Siegel. (MGM). *Cast:* Frank Sinatra, Dean Martin, Shirley MacLaine, Martha Hyer, Arthur Kennedy, Nancy Gates, Steven Peck. *VHS, LD*

Stagecoach

(JOHN FORD, 1939)

Sc.: Dudley Nichols, from the story "Stage to Lordsburg" by Ernest Haycox. *Ph.:* Bert Glennon. *Mus.:* Richard Hageman, W. Franke Harling, John Leipold, Leo Shuken, Louis Gruenberg. *2nd unit dir.:* Yakima Canutt. *Prod.:* John Ford, Walter Wanger. (United Artists). *Cast:* John Wayne, Claire Trevor, Thomas Mitchell, Andy Devine, John Carradine, Donald Meek, Louise Platt, George Bancroft, Berton Churchill, Tim Holt. *VHS, LD*

A Star is Born

(GEORGE CUKOR, 1954)

Sc.: Moss Hart, based on screenplay of 1937 nonmusical film by Dorothy Parker, Alan Campbell, Robert Carson, from story by William Wellman and Carson suggested by 1932 film *What Price Hollywood?* by Gene Fowler and Roland Brown from story by Adela Rogers St. Johns. *Ph.:* Sam Leavitt (Technicolor, CinemaScope). *Col. cons.:* George Hoyningen-Huene. *Prod. des.:* Gene Allen. *Mus.:* Harold Arlen. *Lyr.:* Ira Gershwin. *Chor.:* Richard Barstow. *Prod.:* Sidney Luft. (Warner Bros.). *Cast:* Judy Garland, James Mason, Jack Carson, Charles Bickford, Tommy Noonan. *VHS, LD*

A Streetcar Named Desire

(ELIA KAZAN, 1951)

Sc.: Tennessee Williams, adapted by Oscar Saul from Williams's play. *Ph.:* Harry Stradling. *Mus.:* Alex North. *Prod.:* Charles K. Feldman. (Warner Bros.). *Cast:* Vivien Leigh, Marlon Brando, Kim Hunter, Karl Malden, Rudy Bond, Nick Dennis. *VHS, LD* *

Sullivan's Travels

(PRESTON STURGES, 1941)

Sc.: Preston Sturges. *Ph.:* John B. Seitz. *Mus.:* Leo Shuken, Charles Bradshaw. *Prod.:* Paul Jones. (Paramount). *Cast:* Joel McCrea, Veronica Lake, Robert Warwick, William Demarest, Franklin Pangborn, Porter Hall, Byron Foulger, Margaret Hayes, Eric Blore. *VHS, LD* *

Sunrise

(F. W. MURNAU, 1927)

Sc.: Carl Mayer, from *The Journey to Tilsit* by Hermann Sudermann. *Titl.:* Katharine Hilliker, H. H. Caldwell. *Ph.:* Charles Rosher, Karl Struss. *Mus.:* Hugo Riesenfeld. *Prod. des.:* Rochus Gliese, Edgar G. Ulmer. *Prod.:* Fox Film. *Cast:* George O'Brien, Janet Gaynor, Margaret Livingstone, Bodil Rosing, J. Farrell Macdonald. *VHS*

Sweet Smell of Success

(ALEXANDER MACKENDRICK, 1957)

Sc.: Clifford Odets, adapted by Ernest Lehman from his short story "Tell Me About It Tomorrow." *Ph.:* James Wong Howe. *Mus.:* Elmer Bernstein. *Prod.:* James Hill for Norma-Curtleigh Productions. (United Artists). *Cast:* Burt Lancaster, Tony Curtis, Susan Harrison, Martin Milner, Sam Levene, Barbara Nichols, Jeff Donnell, Edith Atwater, Emile Meyer, Jay Adler. *VHS, LD*

The Tall T

(BUDD BOETTICHER, 1957)

Sc.: Burt Kennedy, from the story "The Captives" by Elmore Leonard. *Ph.:* Charles Lawton, Jr. (color by DeLuxe). *Mus.:* Heinz Roemheld. *Prod.:* Harry Joe Brown. (Columbia). *Cast:* Randolph Scott, Maureen O'Sullivan, Richard Boone, Arthur Hunnicutt, Skip Homeier, Henry Silva. *VHS* *

The Ten Commandments
(CECIL B. DE MILLE, 1923)

Sc.: Jeannie Macpherson. *Ph.:* J. Peverell Marley, Ray Rennahan (sequences in two-strip Technicolor). *Mus.:* Hugo Riesenfeld. *Prod.:* Paramount. *Cast:* Theodore Roberts, James Neill, Estelle Taylor, Charles De Rochefort, Richard Dix, Rod La Rocque, Edythe Chapman, Leatrice Joy. *VHS*

The Ten Commandments
(CECIL B. DE MILLE, 1956)

Sc: Aeneas MacKenzie, Jesse Lasky, Jr., Jack Gariss, Fredric M. Frank. *Ph.:* Loyal Griggs (Technicolor, Vistavision). *Mus.:* Elmer Bernstein. *Prod.:* Cecil B. De Mille. (Paramount). *Cast:* Charlton Heston, Yul Brynner, Anne Baxter, Edward G. Robinson, Yvonne De Carlo, Debra Paget, John Derek, Sir Cedric Hardwicke, Nina Foch, Martha Scott, Judith Anderson, Vincent Price, John Carradine, Olive Deering, Douglas Dumbrille, Henry Wilcoxon, H. B. Warner, Julia Faye. *VHS, LD*

T-Men
(ANTHONY MANN, 1948)

Sc.: John C. Higgins (and uncredited Anthony Mann), from a story by Virginia Kellogg. *Ph.:* John Alton. *Mus.:* Paul Sawtell. *Prod.:* Edward Small for Reliance Pictures. (Eagle-Lion). *Cast:* Dennis O'Keefe, Alfred Ryder, Mary Meade, Wallace Ford, June Lockhart, Charles McGraw, Jane Randolph. *VHS* *

2001: A Space Odyssey
(STANLEY KUBRICK, 1968)

Sc.: Stanley Kubrick, Arthur C. Clarke, from the short story "The Sentinel" by Clarke. *Ph.:* Geoffrey Unsworth (Technicolor-Metrocolor, Super Panavision 70 and Todd-AO); additional photography by: John Alcott. *Spec. photo. eff.:* Douglas Trumbull. *Prod. des.:* Tony Masters, Harry Lange, Ernest Archer. *Prod.:* Stanley Kubrick for Hawk Films. (MGM). Cast: Keir Dullea, Gary Lockwood, William Sylvester, Daniel Richter, Douglas Rain. *VHS, LD*

Two Weeks in Another Town
(VINCENTE MINNELLI, 1962)

Sc.: Charles Schnee, from the novel by Irwin Shaw. *Ph.:* Milton Krasner (Metrocolor, CinemaScope). *Mus.:* David Raksin. *Prod.:* John Houseman. (MGM). *Cast:* Kirk Douglas, Edward G. Robinson, Cyd Charisse, George Hamilton, Dahlia Lavi, Claire Trevor, Rosanna Schiaffino, Mino Doro. *LD* *

Unforgiven
(CLINT EASTWOOD, 1992)

Sc.: David Webb Peoples. *Ph.:* Jack N. Green (Technicolor, Panavision wide screen). *Prod. des.:* Henry Bumstead. *Mus.:* Lennie Niehaus. *Prod.:* Clint Eastwood for Malpaso. (Warner Bros.). *Cast:* Clint Eastwood, Gene Hackman, Morgan Freeman, Richard Harris, Jaime Woolvett, Saul Rubinek, Frances Fisher. *VHS, LD*

The Wedding March
(ERICH VON STROHEIM, 1927)

Sc.: Erich von Stroheim, Harry Carr. *Ph.:* Ben Reynolds, Hal Mohr. *Prod.:* P. A. Powers for the Famous Players-Lasky. (Paramount). *Cast:* Erich von Stroheim, Fay Wray, George Fawcett, Maude George, Cesare Gravina, Dale Fuller, Matthew Betz, Zasu Pitts. *VHS* *

Wild Boys of the Road
(WILLIAM WELLMAN, 1933)

Sc.: Earl Baldwin, from the story "Desperate Youth" by Danny Ahearn. *Ph.:* Arthur Todd. *Prod.:* Darryl F. Zanuck. (First National-Warner Bros.). *Cast:* Frankie Darro, Dorothy Coonan, Edwin Philips, Rochelle Hudson, Ann Hovey, Arthur Hohl, Ward Bond. *

Cecil B. De Mille